BRITAIN'S
LOST LINES

BRITAIN'S LOST LINES

NEW USES FOR FORMER RAILWAY SITES

ANTHONY POULTON-SMITH

The
History
Press

Above: A little luxury in an old railway carriage.
Right: Possibly the most expensive garden sheds in the country.

Back cover image: Courtesy of Amy Rigg.

First published 2015

The History Press
The Mill, Brimscombe Port
Stroud, Gloucestershire, GL5 2QG
www.thehistorypress.co.uk

British Library Cataloguing in Publication Data.
A catalogue record for this book is available from the British Library.

ISBN 978 0 7509 6055 7

Typesetting and origination by The History Press
Printed in China

CONTENTS

INTRODUCTION

Just when Britain's railway network reached its peak is a matter for debate. Examining passenger numbers, freight, the revenue, or miles of track gives different dates and still a peak will not reveal itself. As first Benjamin Disraeli and later Mark Twain reminded us with the phrase, 'Lies, Damned Lies, and Statistics', almost anything can be proven by mathematics.

Most agree any peak will fall somewhere either side of the First World War. By the time the four great railway companies had united under the banner of British Rail, the infrastructure was already in need of significant investment. Later, the infamous cuts of the so-called Beeching Report saw a third of Britain's stations and over 15,000 miles of track removed from the railway system. As nature reclaimed the embankments and cuttings, civilisation soon moved in to reclaim the buildings and goods yards now left empty.

We Brits are a nostalgic bunch and very proud of our railways. Quite rightly so, for whilst our navies were the strength for early empire, later it was the technology of railways which perpetuated British influence and kept much of the map of the globe that pink colour of the Empire (for those who are old enough to recall). Yet line and station closures did not leave us feeling overly melancholy for long. As the 1970s came in, so did the beginnings of the many heritage lines we enjoy today.

As other uses were found for the buildings, old sidings and former marshalling yards, the British sense of humour soon came to the fore. Yet, as we shall see in the following pages, while some examples were deliberate, this was not always the case.

Note: all images are from the author's collection unless otherwise credited.

Abbey Foregate Station in Shrewsbury clearly shows the platform edge with the buildings at the far end.

Aber Bargoed in Gwent has seen its former station put to two uses. Part has been landscaped with the remainder used for the local bypass.

Abergavenny Brecon Road station in Monmouthshire is now home to a doctor's practice.

Aberlour station has been utilised as the modern Speyside Way Visitor Centre, with the railway buildings also doubling up as a tea shop. This route follows the River Spey through Banffshire, Morayshire and Inverness-shire and is one of four long-distance routes in Scotland beginning at Aviemore and ending at Buckpool Harbour in Buckie, a distance of some 65 miles.

Aboyne station in Aberdeenshire has seen the trackbed become a part of the Deeside Way, while the station site is now home to a row of shops on the aptly named Station Square, and includes a chemist and a tandoori restaurant.

Aboyne station houses a number of shops. (*Courtesy of Stan Howe*)

Old Station Fishers, Addingham.

Acrefair in Wales is now an industrial estate with access via a road which was once the trackbed.

Addingham in West Yorkshire has a large building proudly proclaiming it is Old Station Fisheries. This is only partly true; historically this was the site of the railway bridge and not the station proper, which was 200 yards along from here.

Adlestrop bench and original station sign.

Station Road, Adlington, where some of the buildings on the right once served the station.

Adlington in Lancashire closed in 1971, all that remains is Station Road and the former ticket office now known as the White Bear Marina Café. The name comes from the canal and the local pub.

Akeld in Northumberland is one of a number of stations which have been given over to holiday accommodation.

Aldeburgh in Suffolk is the site of a grassy traffic island. Situated at the point where Victoria Road, Saxmundham Road, Leiston Road, and Church Farm Road intersect, the island marks the exact spot where the former railway station once stood.

Alford Town in Lincolnshire closed in the 1960s, the station building but one comprising the aptly named Beechings Way Industrial Estate. Among the diverse businesses were the printing presses of John White and a huge selection of building supplies from Jackson's Building Centres.

Algakirk and Sutterton in Lincolnshire may have been constructed to bring the railway to the village but today the trackbed has become a carriageway, with a roundabout constructed where the A16 and A17 roads converge.

Allendale in Northumberland has been cleared and is now the Allendale Caravan Park.

Allerston in North Yorkshire is near Pickering, famously the southern terminus of the North Yorkshire Moors heritage railway. Any plans this highly successful line may have had to extend further south were effectively scuppered by the development of housing. Allerston is 5 miles away and the site of the station is quite obvious from the rolling stock which is still in situ. The three carriages, all built at Derby in the late 1960s, have been converted to provide delightful self-catering accommodation.

Alton is a name associated with the theme park of Alton Towers. The rides were constructed around the estate, once served by the North Staffordshire Railway on the Churnet Valley line. Today the Landmark Trust has refurbished the station to provide holiday accommodation for up to eight people. The original Italianate style of the exterior has been retained, but inside an instantly recognisable post-war British station has been faithfully reproduced.

Alton station and trackbed.

Annan Shawhill station in the county of Dumfries and Galloway is now a private residence. Here it is the trackbed which interests us, for it now carries a pipeline for the waste water from the Chapelcross nuclear power station.

Appleby East in Cumbria is still largely recognisable as a station and home to a scrap metal dealer.

Arddleen station is today a private residence, and all signs of the track are now buried beneath the A483 towards Welshpool, now that it has been straightened and the railway bridge dismantled. Interestingly, the building shows not a single sign of railway architecture and is thought to predate the arrival of the railway in 1863. It was most likely used by those associated with the Montgomeryshire canal, which was built between 1794 and 1821.

Ardingly in West Sussex was utilised by Hanson Aggregates almost immediately after the station's closure. Initially freight continued to be carried on the railway but, since, the lines have been severed. The company continues to use the station buildings as offices.

Armley Canal Road station building is still standing and is used by a commercial outlet. It has to be said, the oversized sign declaring this is Armley Canal Road is garish in the extreme, white lettering on a red background is not reminiscent of the railway history of the place.

Arthington in West Yorkshire has had two stations. One is now a private residence, while the second helps to serve the new Otley branch line. The junction here formed a triangle, and while two sides have long gone, the area is still known as 'The Triangle' locally. Within that triangle can be found a small building which houses the equipment controlling the local gas supply.

Ashbourne in Derbyshire has been utilised by several more recent concerns. The station site itself is now the car park for Ashbourne Leisure Centre, while the goods yard can be found by locating the new St Oswalds Hospital. The goods shed still stands has a Grade II listing, and today is home to a steel merchant.

Avonwick in Devon saw its station building soon used as a private residence. However, the owners paid homage to the building's original use by utilising the station canopy as the basis for their conservatory.

Ashby-de-la-Zouch station.

Axbridge in Somerset still has its old railway station, and is now home to the local youth club. Outside the building is still accessed via Station Road, while the line of the track is occupied by the Axbridge Bypass (A371).

Aylesbury in Buckinghamshire is now used as an office block and retail park.

Bala in Gwynedd has been cleared and is now home to the local fire station. Unfortunately the demolition included the goods shed which, owing to objections from a local landholder, was constructed so as to appear to be a small castle complete with battlements and turrets.

Ballater station was the stepping-off point for royals heading for Balmoral. Queen Victoria had her own waiting room; this now houses a visitor centre, itself including a replica of Victoria's royal carriage.

Bala station. (*Courtesy of Dr Ben Brooksbank*)

Balquhidder railway station.
(*Courtesy of Dr Ben Brooksbank*)

Balquhidder station was due to close in November 1965 but effectively ceased to provide a service from September following a landslide in Glen Ogle. Today the site has been laid out as a holiday park with a choice of log cabins, caravans, and a camping area.

Barcombe Mills station in Sussex closed in 1969, but preservation work began in 1985 when purchased by Allan Slater. This is no heritage line but there is a station which now serves as the Wheeltappers Restaurant and Tea Room. The old stationmaster's house is a private residence, and in 2003 two cottages were built as holiday accommodation. The Lavender Line could possibly extend through to Barcombe once more and in 2011 such plans included the possible building of a new station building.

Barnoldswick station in West Yorkshire is now home to a supermarket, while the town's war memorial was removed from and brought here to stand at what had once been the platform gates.

Barnsley Court House in South Yorkshire was in use until it was demolished in the 1970s and became the site of Barnsley's famous open-air market. So successful was the site, remembered for its 'Barnsley for Bargains' slogan, the purpose-built market used the same site.

The former Barcombe station, now a holiday let.

Barnstaple Town Quay station became the town's bus station until, in 1999, a purpose-built bus station took over the role a short distance away, and since then the station has been taken over by a café.

Barnstaple Town in Devon saw the signalbox used as a museum until the mid-1990s, while the station building became a restaurant. Today the signal box stands empty, but the station houses a school.

Barnstaple Victoria Road station closed but something of the platforms remains alongside the A39 as the car park for the electricity provider. However, it is on the other side of the road where the surprise is found, here the former goods shed survives as the Grosvenor church. Opened in 1995, there are a number of rooms within given over to private prayer, services, dance, and a number of groups.

Barrington in Cambridgeshire has a single railway carriage offering first-class self-catering accommodation.

Bath Green Park station was originally known as Bath Queen Square, a reference to the prestigious square just a short walk away, but changed its

Grosvenor church in Barnstaple.

name in 1954. Its distinctive glass roof was damaged during a bombing raid in April 1942 and was never replaced by British Rail. Following closure in 1971, it was another decade before Sainsbury's occupied the site of the station with smaller shops operating out of the station buildings. Today the booking hall is home to Green Park Brasserie, while the expanse of the station concourse makes for the perfect covered market, where traders and a farmers' market are regular Saturday events. The space also sees performances associated with the Bath Fringe Festival, while the lower floors are home to local charities and businesses.

Bayards Park at Waverley in Surrey is remembered as much for its floral achievements as it is the railway, although the two are very much linked. The BBC filmed an early television version of *The Railway Children* in 1957, when Geoff Birdfield acted as both signalman and station porter. He later won prizes for his dahlias, of which there were more than 1,000 grown here and numbering over 200 different varieties. Closing the line in 1965 made no difference for Mr Birdfield, who constructed a greenhouse measuring 52ft in length and 12ft wide on the platform, with a cold frame straddling the trackbed. He continued to work as a signalman here until 1980, giving him a total of forty-four years unbroken service to the railways. When the building was finally auctioned off in 1973 the owners restored it to its original condition and now a local preservation society organises annual tours on a walk where some 150 or more individuals are seen.

Beauchief station just outside Sheffield, South Yorkshire, lives on in the nearby Abbeydale Station Hotel later renamed the Beauchief Hotel, while the station site proper is now occupied by a nursing home.

Beal station in Northumberland closed, along with so many others, with the so-called Beeching Axe of the 1960s. Today the station site has been landscaped and while the East Coast Main Line still runs near the village, there is nothing of the buildings remaining. However, the landscaping includes an old North East Railway metal warning sign and a Peckett 0-4-0ST steam locomotive.

Bell Busk station in North Yorkshire spent some years as a private residence following closure. However, today it is one of a number of old railway buildings which have been converted to a bed and breakfast.

Bexhill-on-Sea station is still a superb sight, albeit no train can arrive here today as the rails are long gone. Inside many of the original building features can still be seen, although the interior is occupied by a pub, a restaurant, and the Gorringes Auction Galleries. The former engine shed is still standing, acting as the focal point of a small industrial estate.

Bexhill-on-Sea's lovely old station.

The interior of the West Station public house at Bexhill-on-Sea.

Opened as the original Birmingham station its Doric splendour is still evident.

Blackamoor in Devon was built at what had been an important crossroads for many years, a pivotal point on the coaching routes. When the station was built the stables were utilised by the railway, but when the line closed the stables were refurbished and is now a family residence.

Blackpool Central station closed and that site is now home to the amusement arcade known as Coral Island.

Blacksboat station is now home to the Speyside Way Visitor Centre, offering information on the history of the 65-mile way and tea and refreshments.

Bledlow in Buckinghamshire closed and today the extended station building offers bed and breakfast. The building is not the only link to the days when the trains stopped here, for the guest house is run by the granddaughter of Percy Smith. Mr Smith was stationmaster here from 1918 to 1950; he was only the third to hold that position and one of the longest serving anywhere.

Coral Island on Blackpool's famous Golden Mile, from where the illuminations are switched on each year, was once home to Blackpool Central station.

Blackpool Central station.
(*Courtesy of Dr Ben Brooksbank*)

Botanic Gardens station in Glasgow closed to passengers in February 1939, but the line remained open until October 1964. The building was unusual; its two domes were always likened to the style of a Russian Orthodox Church, but certainly fitted in with the gardens founded in 1817 (which now boast eight glass houses). Passengers may not have used the station, but retail outlets soon moved in. By the end of the 1960s a café known as The Silver Slipper, a plumber's merchant called Mortons, and the Sgt. Peppers nightclub had found a home here. Sadly a disastrous fire on 22 March 1970 put paid to the building and any further use. Deemed unsafe, what remained of the building was demolished. In 2007 an ambitious scheme to restore the building, complete with nightclub and even a miniature railway, was mooted but was soon crushed by opposition to the idea of creating such a place in a peaceful haven like the gardens, despite being a part of the history of the area. The site is now very much overgrown, although what remains of the underground platforms can still be seen.

Boughton in Nottinghamshire is unusual among the other entries here for while the station and line closed in 1955 and everything was cleared, by August 2009 track had been relaid and opened as the High Marnham Test Track. Now the line is used by Network Rail to test new technologies in the form of trains and on-track plant.

Botanic Gardens station, Glasgow.
(Courtesy of Dr Ben Brooksbank)

Bourne Bridge station at Abington in Cambridgeshire was not closed by Dr Richard Beeching, indeed it seems unlikely if he ever even heard of the name of Bourne Bridge for it numbers amongst the earliest of railways station closures, its last passenger travelling in 1851. Whilst it has never been confirmed there is very good reason to believe the present Railway Inn encompasses much of the original station building and has done since it was constructed shortly after the closure of Bourne Bridge and opened to serve the traffic now arriving and departing the new Pampisford station.

Bovey Tracey in Devon once stood alongside the track but is now sits by the local bypass. Most of the buildings are still present and provide a home for the Dartmoor National Park Authority. Among the strangest sights in the storage area are about a dozen large, but nowhere near life-size, resin dinosaurs. These are part of the stocks of *The Jolly Roger*'s stock of models which include figures of pirates, cowboys, knights, animals (wild and domesticated), and figures from Hollywood, and claim to have everything from coffee beans to full-size elephants.

Boxford in Berkshire closed and everything was swept away save for the station's wooden shelter which still keeps the rain off passengers today – as they wait for the local bus.

Brackley Central in Northamptonshire was always something of a misleading building for, when approached from the road, it appears to be a single-storey building. It is now occupied by a supplier of car tyres. However, this

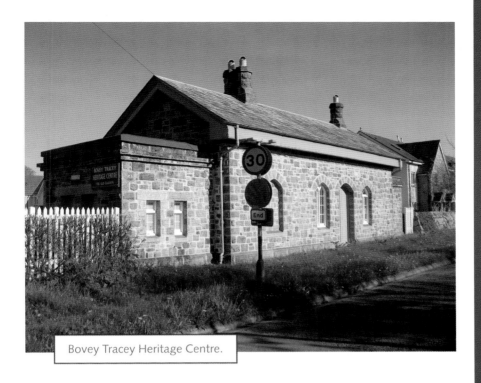

Bovey Tracey Heritage Centre.

Former station shelter, now bus shelter in Boxford.

Fire station and police station at St James' Road, Brackley.

is simply the upper storey of a building which had its foundations at track level and what you see from the road is that part of the building at the top of the cutting.

Bradford's Horton Park station in West Yorkshire may have closed around fifty years ago but the site remained easily recognisable for most of that time until cleared to make way for the Suffa-Tul-Islam University Mosque.

Bramber in West Sussex has one remaining sign of the railway – the carved wooden lettering of the station's name is to be found within an area now belonging to Bramber Garden Nursery.

Bridport West Bay in Dorset first closed in 1916, closed a second time in 1921, again in 1924, and saw its last ever passenger in 1932, although freight continued until 1964. Today the station building houses a café, although even this closed in 2008 before reopening two years later.

Brereton Colliery's trackbed is currently being reworked as the Brereton and Ravenhill Way.

Braunston and Willoughby station site. Note the van in the garden, now a shed, of the old Station House.

This old and dilapidated van is the sole sign of the former Brinklow station in Warwickshire.

Between its life as a railway station and a café, the building can boast being home to the offices of a local boat yard for some ten years between the 1970s and '80s.

Brixham in Devon was the terminus for a branch line from Churston, still the passing loop on the Paignton and Dartmouth heritage line, this station was ostensibly to serve the fishing port before its closure in 1963. Suggestions of reopening the branch are optimistic considering the gaps which now exist in this small branch line. These number actual gaps in the sense of missing bridges and effective gaps where the trackbed is now occupied by the gardens of houses built after the line closed. There is also the school playground and car park to contend with, for Brixham station was demolished and is now home, in part, to Furzeham County Primary School.

Broadstone station in Dorset is now the site of Broadstone Leisure Centre, its car park, and a traffic island.

The local train leaving Churston for Brixham station on the now closed line. (*Courtesy of Dr Ben Brooksbank*)

Brixham station entrance. (*Courtesy of Dr Ben Brooksbank*)

Broadway in Worcestershire closed to passengers in 1960, although express trains continued to come through here for another eight years until the track was lifted. For almost fifty years the only reminders were the bridge across the main road into Broadway and the stationmaster's house, now a guest house. At the time of writing permission has been granted for the Gloucestershire and Warwickshire Heritage Railway to rebuild a station and relay the track to bring the line here, with a service running in 2016.

Brompton Road on the London Underground closed in 1934. During the Second World War it became a (then) secret command centre, but has recently been sold by the Ministry of Defence and a developer has successfully applied to turn this building into apartments.

Burnham Market in Norfolk first saw its post-railway usage as a garage called Burnham Motors. Shortly before the third millennium it became a part of the Hoste Arms Hotel, thereafter the Railway Inn, with a railway carriage (as well as the old station) offering excellent accommodation.

Burnham-on-Sea in Somerset closed and the platform and goods shed were demolished. Today the station building is occupied by a café known as TA8 (this the first part of the postcode), while across the road we see the Somerset & Dorset public house, this renamed as such to mark the closing of the railway which was on the Somerset and Dorset railway. The extreme south-east part of the site was later developed and was home to the first ever supermarket under the Waitrose banner – it is now owned by a Morrisons – while the trackbed has become Marine Drive and has been a great aid to easing traffic congestion in the resort. To the right and rear of the café is a new Royal National Lifeboat Institute Station. Once the station building had housed the lifeboat, as evidenced by the many images adorning the walls of the new building.

The Lifeboat station at Burnham-on-Sea is now TA8's Bistro and stands on the old railway site.

Burslem station in the Potteries stood alongside Burslem Park. After closure the station was demolished and became part of the park.

Burwell in Cambridgeshire closed in 1965. Today all visible remains are buried under a housing estate where the only reminders are in the form of two street names, Station Gate and Railway Close. However, it is the time shortly after closure which is most interesting as the site was then home to a factory producing cardboard.

Byker station in Newcastle-upon-Tyne is now the car park at the rear of Morrison's supermarket.

Cadeleigh in Devon is now home to the Devon Railway Centre, having turned almost full circle; however, in between it housed the county council until 1997.

Calderdale's North Bridge station in West Yorkshire is now home to the local leisure centre.

Camberwell in London has been converted into a car mechanic's.

Camelford in Cornwall was used as the site of the British Cycle Museum and has given its name to the Camelford Cycle Way.

Carisbrooke station on the Isle of Wight closed in 1953 and the site is now almost invisible within the grounds of the school playing field.

Carrington in Nottinghamshire closed in 1968. Soon afterwards the station buildings were occupied by, among others, a sweet shop and the Alldogs Poodle Parlour. These businesses and buildings are long gone, but with the cutting now filled in, it has become the regional facility of the Open University.

Castle Ashby and Earl's Barton station is still standing and still home to two railway carriages. One stands to the rear of the current building, the second has only one end visible, the other is swallowed up by the building itself – a quite ingenious way to provide an annexe. Until 2013 this was a restaurant known as Dunkley's but has now sadly closed and its future is uncertain.

Catterick Bridge in North Yorkshire was cleared soon after the line closed. Whilst some minor features can just be made out, the site is now part of the waste management site for the district of Richmondshire.

Cheadle Heath in Greater Manchester still has freight trains carrying limestone from the Peak District, yet there is no sign of the station for it is buried beneath a new Morrison's supermarket and its car park.

Cheddar in Somerset kept its station buildings which are now occupied by office units.

Chester Liverpool Road was used by a coal merchant shortly after closure in the 1970s, but since the turn of the twenty-first century has been home to a fitness centre.

Chesterfield Market Place was a large and expensive development when first laid out and yet the area has been developed so extensively it is difficult to trace the site on the ground with any accuracy, although traces can be seen in the car park of the Portland Hotel.

Chudleigh station in Devon closed to passengers in 1958 and to freight nine years later, although only coal came through here during the last two years. Today the busy A38 runs straight through the now-cleared station site, however, it is easy to find the place as the junction on the carriageway is known as Chudleigh Station.

Chwilog in Gwynedd is today occupied by the village bus station.

Cleckheaton in Yorkshire is undoubtedly a unique case and while it would be difficult to see the use of the site as unusual, it certainly has a most extraordinary story. Opened in 1848 and taking traffic from Heckmondwike, Low Moor and Mirfield as part of the Lancashire and Yorkshire Railway, in 1922 it was absorbed by the London and North Western Railway, the London, Midland and Scottish in 1923, and nationalised shortly after the

Second World War. The last passenger train arrived here at 23:21 on 12 June 1965, with the last freight train passing through four years later.

Our interest comes from a case heard at Wakefield Crown Court on 24 April 1972. In the dock stood a Dewsbury man charged, as the prosecution stated, with 'Stealing Cleckheaton Station'. It soon transpired that British Rail had issued a contract for the clearing of this land in August of the previous year. As was normal, the materials and scrap would become the property of the contractors and whatever monies they gleaned from its disposal was theirs. Yet when the contractors arrived they discovered the work had already been done and Cleckheaton station was no more. An investigation revealed how, three weeks earlier, the man in the dock had headed the team which had been given a similar contract and had quickly disposed of the site and all the contents. This contract had been issued by another company, not British Rail who owned the property. It was decided the defendant had acted in good faith, had not broken any laws, and was found not guilty. Furthermore, it was said he had been as much a victim as everyone else and had indeed lost a significant amount of cash on the deal. All subsequent attempts to trace the company who had issued the contract to him met with failure.

Cliddesden in Hampshire was, when open, marked by a wind engine which supplied power to both the station and the railway cottages. This landmark outlasted the railway which closed in 1934. A train stopped here in 1937, although the station had been renamed Buggleskelly for the 1937 British film *Oh, Mr Porter!* starring Will Hay.

Cloughton north of Scarborough in North Yorkshire closed in the 1960s and the route is now a part of the Cinder Trail. This station, always among the most attractive when the line was open with its award-winning floral displays, has been completely renovated and now boasts a tearoom, with guest accommodation in the the former goods shed, a converted railway carriage, and the station buildings themselves.

Clowne South in Derbyshire has seen many changes but the station buildings remain. The stationmaster's house has recently undergone restoration and is now a business centre, while the booking hall has been used by both a bank and a shop selling bridal wear.

Coalville Town closed in 1964 and the building still stands, today home to a children's nursery.

Former stationmaster Alfred Hart could still be as proud of the immaculate gardens at Cloughton station today as when he was a prizewinner on many occasions.

What was the old Coalbrookdale station is now the Green Woods Centre.

Coalport station in Shropshire.

Cockermouth in Cumbria closed in 1966, the station buildings have been demolished and the Cockermouth Mountain Rescue and Cumbria Fire Service Headquarters buildings now occupy the site.

Coleford Great Western Railway Museum in Gloucestershire.

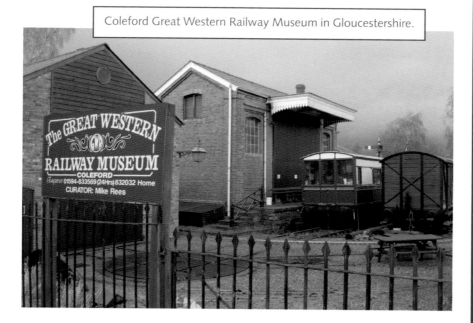

C

Coleford's GWR Museum occupies the old station site.

Collingham Bridge near Leeds in West Yorkshire saw the former coal yard now covered with tarmac to provide car parking for those using facilities on the River Wharfe.

Corwen station in Denbighshire became a showroom for the well-known company Ifor Williams Trailers.

Coundon Road in Coventry, West Midlands closed in 1965. The station-master's house still exists and is now owned by Bablake School and used as their foundation's uniform shop.

Countesthorpe has little unusual evidence, save for the public house known as the Railway Inn and one or two roads which bear names showing their legacy. While that of Station Road is most predictable, that of Beechings Close comes as something of a surprise. It is easy to see how the developers of the estate used 'Close' in a rather tongue-in-cheek way to point to Baron Beeching. However, little homework was done here for the good doctor never got the opportunity to close Countesthorpe station, as by the time the report was released in March 1963 the station had already been gone for fourteen months.

The old station buildings, these days a private residence, at Compton in Berkshire where an industrial estate now occupies the former goods yard.

Countesthorpe, Leicestershire – Beechings Close was cut on the former station yard.

Cowbit in Lincolnshire has seen a number of uses for the buildings, some commercial, others as private residences. However, it is the waiting shelter on the opposite platform to the main building which attracts our attention, for here we find a dog-grooming parlour aptly named Paws at the Station.

Cowes on the Isle of Wight is a place synonymous with the sea, but it is the former railway station which interests us here, the building now housing a Co-op supermarket.

Cranleigh in Surrey closed in 1965 and shortly afterwards the site was demolished. Now all signs are buried beneath the Stocklund Square housing and shopping centre development.

Crianlarich in Stirling closed in 1965, the site was next home to a lumber yard, while today the station building houses the Crianlarich Community Centre.

The platform edge is still visible at the rear of the shops at Stocklund Square, Cranleigh.

Croydon Central station opened and closed in the nineteenth century and little of the station remains, save for a retaining wall for the cutting which is now a part of neighbouring Queen's Gardens. The station site itself is now occupied by the Town Hall.

Cullompton station in Devon is probably a name familiar to drivers who use the southern end of the M5 motorway with any regularity as it is also the name of the services off the M5. Today trains still pass adjacent to the services which occupy the very site of the former station and yard.

Curzon Street in Birmingham was the original terminus of the line from Euston station in London. A look at this splendid building is enough to see why, following its closure in 1966, the place has been used on several occasions to display art collections. The area where the line and sidings are seen is still undeveloped, currently used in part as a car park, but has been earmarked as the terminus for the new HS2 rail link.

Cullompton Services, the tracks still run alongside.

The architecture of the station building will soon be seen at the other end of the original line to the nation's capital, for the redevelopment of Euston station has provided the very real opportunity for the rebuilding of the Euston Arch, the first great monument of the railway age. Some twenty-four stones have been recovered from Prescott Channel, a tributary of the River Lea, when the riverbed was dredged during preparations for the 2012 Olympics.

Cwmbran in Gwent has its present-day railway station on the opposite side of the town from where the former railway station stood on Victoria Road. It is now the site of a doctor's practice and car park.

Dartmouth station in Devon was built by Isambard Kingdom Brunel at the end of the nineteenth century. Today the ornate wooden building survives as the Station Restaurant, although only the exterior has any reminders of the railway; inside the decor has a maritime theme with the emphasis on fishing.

It may come as a surprise to discover that, station or not, Dartmouth has never seen a single train any closer than at Kingswear directly opposite here over the River Dart. It was Brunel's plan to bring the line here from Torbay via a bridge crossing the Dart. Opposition to the bridge spoiling the stunning scenery of the Dart Valley resulted in the Dartmouth service being abandoned and all traffic taken to Kingswear and thereafter crossing the river by ferry or floating bridge. This was bad news for the stationmaster at Dartmouth who was earning a good deal more than his counterpart at Kingswear, owing to the potential importance of the service – many of the passengers would have been travelling to what is now the Royal Naval College, Dartmouth, but was then HMS *Britannia*.

To this day no bridge can be constructed over the Dart below Totnes – the Brutus Bridge, opened here in 1982, is the lowest possible crossing. This also makes Dartmouth station one of the few stations in the world never to have seen a train or even a rail.

Dartmouth station has never seen a train.

Delabole in Cornwall was used as much for the local quarry as for passengers. While the station building is now in private ownership, the former engine shed is still recognisable, although today it is the local fire station and houses the fire engine – not a steam one.

Dent station stands 1,150ft above sea level, situated on the famous Settle–Carlisle route it is the highest mainline station in the country. Delightfully refurbished, it now offers quality self-catering accommodation for visitors.

Dersingham in Norfolk closed in 1969 and the station's buildings have been used as offices and storage for a builder's merchant.

Devonport Kings Road in Plymouth was closed in 1964. City College was built here, a partner of the University of Plymouth. Ironically, considering the great clouds of smoke billowing from steam locomotives over the years, the college is one of the most successful participants in the 10:10 project and over the course of a single year cut their carbon emissions by a highly laudable 38 per cent.

Delabole fire
station occupies
the old goods shed.

Donnington station in Shropshire closed in 1964 and the site is now occupied by the Wyevale Garden Centre.

Dudley in the West Midlands was closed in 1964 and all the buildings were demolished three years later. However, rail returned in the shape of the country's first freightliner terminal until that also closed. Today there is talk of the site being developed for housing, unless the planned state of the art football stadium comes to fruition. Until then the region is given over to walkers, bird-watchers, and dog owners.

Dudley Port Lower Level station in the West Midlands was virtually freight-only from 1887 until 1964 when it closed completely. Views from the canal viaduct, which runs parallel to the High level line, shows the overgrown line still has its rails *in situ* while the scrap metal dealers occupy the station forecourt with a small office building opposite.

Duddeston station with the sheds at the rear, alongside the disused platforms and tracks.

Dudley Port Lower Level has no passengers, but the rails are still *in situ*.

Dudley Port Upper Level still serves passengers.

Earl's Barton in Leicestershire has, until recently, been occupied by Dunkley's Restaurant.

Extra seating was offered at Dunkley's Restaurant by a former carriage.

Dunmow at Great Dunmow in Essex closed and all remains have been obliterated – even the trackbed is now used by the B1256 Dunmow bypass.

Dunstable North has had every sign of the station bulldozed and is now home to the offices of South Bedfordshire District Council.

Earswick station in North Yorkshire was cleared and a pub now occupies the site. With a railway signal still standing outside the premises and a sign accurately depicting the name, the Flag & Whistle public house, is a lasting reminder of its history.

The Flag & Whistle at Earswick, North Yorkshire.

East Anstey in Devon closed in the 1960s and today both station building and goods shed have been converted into private residences. This is not the only time the station has been used for other purposes. In 1944 Ealing Studios used the site when filming *The Halfway House*.

Ebberston in North Yorkshire is around 8 miles away from a railway line today. It has now been refurbished to create two self-catering apartments, but is still very recognisabe as an old railway property.

Edinburgh Princes Street station closed in 1965 and was demolished by the end of the decade. The Caledonian Hotel remains open, while a major office development was constructed on the site of the parcels office in the 1990s.

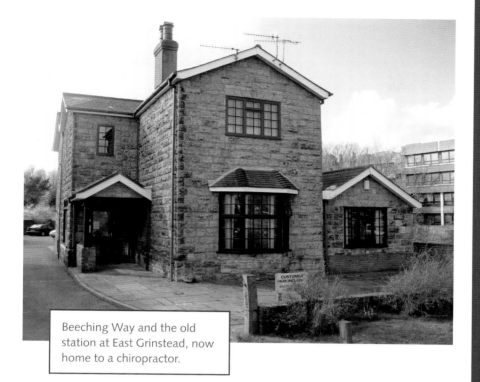

Beeching Way and the old station at East Grinstead, now home to a chiropractor.

Egginton Junction in Derbyshire may have closed but the line remained *in situ* and is used by British Rail Research as a test track. The station was utilised by a caravan dealer.

Egloskerry in Cornwall closed to all traffic in 1996. With the trackbed between the platforms filled in chances of reopening the line seem remote, but plans have not be abandoned entirely.

Correctly known as the Egloskerry Old Station Bed and Breakfast, there are two rooms available as accommodation – the Padstow Room and the Atlantic Coast Express Room. The latter fittingly recalls the holiday train which left Waterloo and split at Exeter, Okehampton and Halwill Junction. This enabled tourists to reach their ultimate destinations of Plymouth, Ilfracombe, Bude and, on this particular line, Padstow. The overall journey from Waterloo to Padstow amounted to 260 miles.

The station itself retains much of the original features and is still recognisable as a West Country railway station, even if the station sign is not visible. At the close of the twentieth century a Parcels and Miscellaneous Van was dropped in by a crane; it now stands on a short length of track reinstated between the old platforms after the soil in-fill had been removed solely for that purpose. Within the owners display a selection of memorabilia relevant to Egloskerry's railway link. Among the images and items from a bygone era is the old station lamp. Complete with the station's name, it was brought all the way from London in person by a gentleman who had purchased it specifically to return it to Egloskerry.

Egloskerry's station guesthouse.

Ellon in Aberdeenshire has little remaining. The trackbed of the main line is now part of the long-distance footpath known as the Formartine and Buchan Way, whilst the branch line has housing which is part of Hospital Road.

Embsay in North Yorkshire is today a part of the Yorkshire Dales Railway heritage line, running from here to Bolton Abbey. In March 2004 the station was used as the backdrop for the fictional Hotten station in the ITV soap opera *Emmerdale*.

Endon and Stockton Brook station still has tracks and a level crossing.

Ettington in Warwickshire has little remaining to show it was ever a part of the railway system. Today the site is occupied by a timber merchant and stables.

Etwall in Derbyshire became home to an agricultural engineering company.

Evercreech and **Evercreech Junction** have both been utilised in an area of Somerset which is predominantly rural. They were featured in a 1963 documentary presented by poet and railway enthusiast Sir John Betjeman. When the line closed three years later what had been the Station Inn public house was renamed the Silent Whistle. By the end of the 1970s new owners decided this unique name had to go and since then this has been known by the uninspired name of the Natterjack. Just a short distance away is the former goods yard, now home to an industrial estate where one building still shows evidence of its history.

Evercreech Junction industrial estate.

Fakenham East in Norfolk may eventually become a part of the Mid-Norfolk heritage line, but the station will not be on the original site as this is now been occupied by sheltered housing.

Fallowfield station in Manchester has been put to good use since its closure. The station building became a public house called Remedy, while the goods yard saw the construction of an apartment block, a Sainsbury's and a public car park.

Fernhill Heath in Worcestershire was opened in February 1852 when it was known as Fearnhall Heath. It changed to its present name in 1883 and remained so until it closed in April 1965. Nothing remains of the station, the footbridge seen here today was never a part of the station but built over the still-open line to enable passengers to cross. Oddly when the station was open the only method of accessing the platform on the opposite side was by crossing the line by means of a walk-over crossing.

The bridge crossing the railway, which was never here when the station at Fernhill Heath was in use.

Folkestone Harbour station stood at the end of a viaduct between the inner and outer harbours. The question remains as to whether the track was laid on the existing harbour walls or whether the two were planned to exist together. Recent plans to reopen and develop the site have fallen by the

Flyers Way industrial estate.

wayside and at the time of writing it appears the track will be lifted, the viaduct demolished and the harbour effectively closed.

Fordham in Cambridgeshire was originally used by a contractor of roofing and scaffolding, and later for waste management. In the twenty-first century it seems the county council are planning to utilise this place for a recycling centre.

The viaduct leading to Folkestone Harbour station.

Forest Row station near Wealden in East Sussex retains a glimpse of the platforms, but it is the goods shed which has a new lease of life, as the original building on what is now the local industrial estate.

Formby Power station railway closed in 1944, two years before the power station itself. Later the station was used by the firm, Metal Closures Rosslite Ltd, whose factory produced expanded polystyrene products for packaging and insulation.

Frittenden Road station at Headcorn in Kentstill has part of the base of the building and much of the platform in existence, albeit the latter very much overgrown. The former trackbed is straddled by a joinery business.

Frittenden Road at Headcorn, the platform edge can be made out on the left.

Gedling and Carlton station in Nottinghamshire has seen the station building become home to a youth hostel.

Girtford Hall in Bedfordshire has been cleared and the best marker to the site of this halt is the traffic island on Georgetown Road, near the London Road Industrial Estate.

Gisburn station in Lancashire closed in the 1960s but left a lasting mark on the local map. It is difficult to understand just how much power the railways wielded in those early days, but an insight can be seen when we realise the town's name changed from Gisburne to Gisburn simply because the railway timetable and station sign omitted the final 'e'. It seems it was easier to change the name of the place than change the mind of the railway company.

Glan Llyn Halt in Gwynedd closed in 1965 and the station became a part of the Bala Lake Railway, a narrow-gauge line opened along the trackbed of the closed line. The halt, even for the heritage line, has very limited use and indeed sees more traffic in the winter months when the station is used as the grotto on their Santa Specials.

Glastonbury and Street in Somerset closed in 1965 and the site is now occupied by a timber yard. Note the level crossing gates at the entrance are not original, unlike the canopy from the railway station which was removed and now serves as a shelter for the market at Glastonbury.

Grange Road station, Crawley Down, West Sussex, had all buildings demolished and now houses a parade of shops, with flats available on the upper floors, and a new medical centre.

Granville Street near Five Ways in Birmingham, the station may have gone but the trackbed is still evidently in use (albeit unofficially).

Greenwich Park in London closed in 1928, but the station building survived as recently as the 1960s, in the interim it housed a billiard hall and later the offices of a building company.

Grimston in Leicestershire saw closure of the station in 1957 although through traffic continued for another twelve years. It was then that the track was adapted as the Old Dalby Test Track, firstly to test the Advanced Passenger Train and thereafter its successor, the Class 390 Pendolino.

Grimstone and Frampton station in Dorset closed in 1966. The station site was cleared and Minster Fuels quickly occupied the site, the company becoming part of the Watson Group in 2009.

Hammerwich station is no longer visible, although some rails have been lifted to the west, within a few yards of the site, and at least one track (and occasionally both) can be seen *in situ* to the east. The footbridge across the line(s) is not only still intact but is in use almost daily. It is mainly a means to gain access to the fields beyond, principally for dog owners, although there does not seem to be any evidence that this was ever a public thoroughfare, other than as a means to cross the line.

Handsworth and Smethwick station in the West Midlands reopened in 1999 as Handsworth Booth Street, a stop on the newly opened tram route between Birmingham Snow Hill and Wolverhampton.

Hartington in Derbyshire was soon turned into a footpath and cyclepath, indeed what is now known as the Tissington Trail was one of the very first to see the potential for these easy gradients to be used for such. However, it is Ashbourne Tunnel which really stands out here. Closed for some years it now affords easier access to Ashbourne, but passing through will trigger a recording which, unless you are aware of it, can be quite disconcerting

Hammerich Station Road and the view of one line from the footbridge, the track is still *in situ* for at least half a mile.

Hammerwich Station Road Station, where some of the rails are still around and the footbridge is still in use as part of an unofficial footpath.

Handsworth Booth Street tram stop.

when hearing the sound of a steam locomotive pulling a train echoing along the tunnel.

Hassop in Derbyshire stands on the Monsal Trail. Visitors can hire a bicycle to travel the former trackbed, which includes three reopened tunnels, from what was the station. The building also houses a café, gift shop, and a bookshop, all quite far removed from the original use of the place which was to serve the Dukes of Devonshire at Chatsworth House, indeed it was originally known as Hassop for Chatsworth.

Hathern in Nottinghamshire closed in 1960 and the station buildings are now utilised by an engineering workshop and a recording studio.

Hawsker in North Yorkshire now stands on the footpath and cycle path known as the Cinder Trail, so-called because the track was laid on a bed of cinders instead of the normal ballast. The station now houses a cycle hire business, whilst accommodation is provided courtesy of a refitted coach.

Hayle in Cornwall has a single 1950s-style railway carriage, one suitably refitted to provide self-catering accommodation.

Today, the platform at the former Hassop station remains obvious, if a little overgrown, and the trackbed the perfect cycle path with its gentle gradients.

The unmistakable image of a rural railway station can be seen at Hawsker where self-catering accommodation and cycle hire are available.

Heathfield in East Sussex is now occupied by an industrial estate and public car park, while the booking office is now home to a shop and a café.

Helmshore in Lancashire closed in the 1960s and has been swept away as the area has been developed. One reminder of the railway remains, however, as the former signal box is now a private residence.

Henfield in West Sussex was cleared soon after closure, although the trackbed still carries the Downs Link footpath. The station site itself still includes Station Road and has been developed as the ironically named Beechings Estate.

Heathfield station, now home to the Steamer Cookshop and Café.

Hermitage Green in Berkshire has seen the sidings and much of the station site given over to a housing development. Work continued over several decades and was only completed in 2007.

Hinton in Worcestershire was not closed until 1963 and yet it found another use during the Second World War when it became a military fuel dump. It was the victim of at least one unsuccessful bombing raid. Following closure,

This quiet residential area was once a bustling yard at Hermitage Green.

several companies used this area, including the Midlands Electricity Board who used it as a storage facility.

Holbeach in Lincolnshire closed to trains fifty years ago but, in the twenty-first century, the area is finally being redeveloped with the station building having been converted into flats.

Holmsley in Hampshire no longer has a track, indeed the line is now buried beneath the Burley to Brockenhurst road. The platforms are still evident, as is the station house, which is now a restaurant serving delicious cream teas.

Horncastle in Lincolnshire has little evidence of having been a railway site, save for a single warehouse. Today this is home to the Bush Tyres organisation, while the remainder has become the Granary Way Housing Estate, itself a reminder of the kind of cargo this rural station could have expected to handle.

Horsbridge in Hampshire has had a chequered past since its closure in September 1967. At first the site was derelict – bricks and tiles disappeared

Holmsley's former station, now a tea room.

from the station buildings, presumably to enjoy a new life in some DIY project, while the signalbox was dismantled and taken away to an unknown location. Now in a state of disrepair the station building has been used by the local fire brigade who employed it in their practise exercises, not that it was ever on fire, they simply repeatedly fell through the floor!

In 1985 a buyer paid £50,000 for the station and began converting the property into a delightful two-bedroomed property – although Hampshire County Council stipulated this was on the understanding the gap between the two platforms could never be utilised as the beginnings of a swimming pool. The station, now very much restored to its Victorian-like appearance, does have tracks once more. These hold a Southern Railway passenger carriage bought for £1,500 which now serves as the dining room.

Horsmonden in Kent has been used as a garage appropriately named the Old Station Garage.

Hunstanton in Norfolk has seen the station turned into a large car and coach park. However, here it is the coal shed which interests us. In 2008 it opened as an art gallery, the first exhibition fittingly displaying memorabilia and photographs of the line between King's Lynn and Hunstanston.

Horsmonden in Kent, now the Old Station Garage.

Hulme End station is now the Manifold Valley Visitor Centre.

The Tea Junction is a refurbished engine shed at Hulme End station.

Ilkeston North station in Derbyshire was cleared following closure and even the bridges were filled in. In later years the trackbed became home to the Cotmanhay Linear Park. The station and yard have been home to Ilkeston's police station since the 1990s.

Ilkeston Town station in Derbyshire was situated at the end of Chalons Way near the large Tesco supermarket, with the track roughly following the line of what is now Millership Way.

Ingrow East station near Bradford in West Yorkshire had a large goods yard to service the local mills. Today both station and yard are occupied by a branch of builder's merchants Travis Perkins.

Viaduct at John O'Gaunt.

Kelvin Hall Station in Glasgow closed in 1964. The buildings then doubled as both a workshop and an auction house before lying empty for some time. Due to their dilapidated condition they were demolished in 2007, leaving the site as empty as the neighbouring goods yard since it was vacated by a scrap metal dealer.

Keswick in Cumbria may be closed but the station building remains as a hotel.

Kibworth in Leicestershire became home to a timber merchant and fencing supplier shortly after its closure in the late 1960s.

Kidlington in Oxfordshire lost its train service in 1964, but the station buildings soon found a new lease of life. Firstly a printing business occupied the building, this was succeeded by a plastics company, who gave way to a retailer of antiques, and then a company who advertised their services repairing dentures. As with so many goods yards, a small industrial estate grew on what became known as Station Field.

Kidsgrove Liverpool Road in Staffordshire closed in 1964. While the trains still bypass the site, the station and yard are now occupied by a large Tesco supermarket.

Kielder station in Northumberland is now a private house, but the neighbouring building acts as a reminder because it is still known as Station Garage. Opened as Kielder it was renamed Kielder Forest in 1948. The reservoir known as Kielder Water was flooded in 1982 after seven years of construction. Among the areas flooded was the former trackbed east of the station which is now under many feet of water.

Kildwick and Crosshills in North Yorkshire closed in 1965 and the site cleared. The goods yard now houses the local council and their materials required for road repairs.

Kimberley West in Nottinghamshire closed to passenger traffic as early as 1917, although goods continued to come here until 1951. The station house still stands, albeit derelict, previously housing Kimberley Ex-Servicemen's Club and Kimberley Social Club.

Kineton in Warwickshire is now occupied by the Plantagenet Trading Estate. Whilst the name may be appropriate for this historical area it hardly recognises the earlier use by the railway.

Kiplingcotes in the East Riding of Yorkshire closed in late 1965. All the station buildings and platform survive, indeed with the return of the rails and sleepers it would be difficult to tell it has been fifty years since any rail traffic was seen. The track is now a walking route, with a number of small businesses occupying the station building and stationmaster's house. Even the old signal box has a new lease of life as a gallery.

Kiplingcotes' former signal box is now an art gallery.

Kiplingcotes station, with the platform edge in the foreground.

The platform edge is very clear in what is now the car park for the Royal Lancaster Infirmary.

Langrick in Lincolnshire is home to the Langrick Station Café, itself serving the Water Rail Way, a cycle and footpath along the line of the former railway created by Sustrans. Whether this is the original building or not is hotly disputed, although in either case there is little of the original building left.

Ledbury Town Halt closed in 1959, but can still be traced as part is still well marked as Ledbury Town Trail.

Leeds Central station in West Yorkshire closed in 1967. Since then the site has seen, and continues to see, phases of major redevelopment. Initially a retail park took up residence, this later included a number of office buildings, a Royal Mail sorting office, and the planned development

Ledbury Town Trail.

known as Lumiere. This development was to dominate the city's skyline. Two towers – thirty-two storeys and 367ft high, and fifty-four storeys and 561ft – sheathed in glass, made the smaller construction appear blue and the larger skyscraper had a red hue. Inside, 20,000 sq. ft of retail space and 10,000 sq. ft of office space would exist alongside some 650 apartments. What would have been the tallest residential skyscraper in Western Europe saw groundwork commence in 2007 and foundation work beginning in early 2008. Financial uncertainty saw the work suspended in July 2008, although the delay was expected to be short-lived and even resulted in an extra storey being added to each building. Sadly the developers went into liquidation in early 2009 and the project was officially cancelled in 2010. Today Travelodge have constructed another of their hotels here, although this soars to just six storeys in height and dwarfed by the multi-storey car park across the road.

Leicester Campbell Street saw a rebuild towards the end of the nineteenth century, improvements resulted in access to the station being from London Road. Some of those original buildings are still put to good use by Royal Mail.

Leicester Central station saw its booking office, platforms and associated buildings demolished in 1970, and small industries replaced the railway property. A car park replaced the site of the signal box and turntable. More recently the surviving station buildings are marked to be restored as part of the city's regeneration scheme of the waterside area. Reminders of the days when trains stopped here can be found in signs and the imagery on the walls, while the former taxi waiting area retains the glass roof and lighting.

Leicester West is an historic site; a station on the Leicester to Swannington line, it was the first route opened in the Midlands and was in operation from 1832. A single signal commemorates the history of a site now given over to a public park known as the Rally.

Lincoln St Marks station is still an imposing building with its portico of iconic design, even though it has not seen a train since 1985. It is now the offices of a chain of kitchenware stores. The site is now home to the St Marks Shopping Centre where a replica signalbox has been erected, ostensibly as a place to hang the old station's signs.

Llandbedrgoch in Anglesey closed in 1930 and everything was removed by 1953. Today this is a caravan site.

What had been Liverpool Road station in Kidsgrove.

Llanberis in Gwynedd has seen the trackbed adapted as the A4086, while the station building is now a craft shop.

Llanerchymedd station on the island of Anglesey closed in 1964 and Anglesey County Council, who own the site, have plans to develop it as a railway museum.

Llanuwchllyn station in Gwynedd closed to passengers in 1972 but reopened seven years later as part of the Bala Light Railway. However, the original station site has also been allocated elsewhere, the cattle dock is now a picnic area, the goods shed is home to a woodworking shop, and what had been a building on platform number two is now an office.

Llanwnda in Gwynedd has no trace of the station remaining, although it is easy enough to locate the site of the station building simply by locating the traffic island where the A487 and A499 intersect.

Llwyngwern in Gwynedd has little reminders of the railway station, save for one small part now doubling as a bus shelter.

Lodge Hill in Somerset closed in 1963, although the buildings were not demolished but removed brick by brick for assembly elsewhere. It is the trackbed which interests us here for, into the twenty-first century, this straight line was in regular use by light aircraft as an airfield.

Longridge in Lancashire is now home to the Longridge Town Council offices and the Old Station Café.

Lord's Bridge station in Cambridgeshire closed in 1968. As if to prove there is no limit to ingenuity when it comes to finding a use for old railway property, we find a station which is now home to the Mullard Radio Astronomy Observatory. The rails are still put to good use, to enable the radio telescope to run along it for around 3 miles, which effectively makes it a 3-mile radio telescope when used in conjunction with others. Built on the so-called Varsity Line between Oxford and Cambridge, the station only existed to serve the lord of the manor and we can only wonder as to what he would have made of the modern use of his station.

Longridge and the former station have been put to good use by the Old Station Café, a small museum and the Town Council.

Lower Edmonton station in London closed in 1964; one of the platforms is still clearly marked by Edmonton Green Shopping Centre.

Low Moor station near Bradford, West Yorkshire closed and in July 1995 a new museum of passenger transport opened here. Known as Transperience it remained open for just two years before closing with debts of over £1 million.

Luton Bute in Bedfordshire soon became indistinguishable from other old station sites and yet another car park was marked out. However, recent developments have seen plans becoming reality as the area is now a part of a guided busway scheme.

Lydd Town in Kent saw its buildings given over to an impromptu car repair centre, but when that went away in the 1980s those buildings became derelict and the area is now used to provide parking for refuse collection vehicles.

Lytham St Annes in Lancashire is now home to a fire station, and the neighbouring Railway Inn is the only remaining indication that there was a line here.

Lytham St Annes Fire Station occupies the station site, in the background the sole reminder of the former railway in the name of the Railway Inn.

Maldon East and Heybridge in Essex closed and the ornate station building was put to good use as a restaurant. Today the still superb building is rather hidden amidst a collection of units on an industrial estate.

Malpas in Cheshire has seen the former station buildings put to good use as offices.

Manchester Central station has been converted into the exhibition and conference centre, appropriately named Manchester Central.

Manchester Liverpool Road station has changed little from the outside, inside it is one of the halls of the famed Manchester Museum of Science and Industry.

Manchester's Liverpool Road station, now a part of the Museum of Science & Industry.

Manor Way station at Beckton in London has disappeared completely beneath the University of East London's Cyprus Campus.

Marazion in Cornwall was formerly home to six coaches used as holiday accommodation. When the station closed four of these coaches were sold on, the two remaining eventually rotted away and the site was cleared. Today the station building has been refurbished as a two-bedroomed bungalow at the centre of some nine holiday cottages.

Marefield Junction in Leicestershire was near to the John O'Gaunt viaduct. This massive brick construction consists of fourteen arches averaging 60ft in height. Today the red brick stands out in the landscape, although no train has crossed here for fifty years, the only activity being the walkers and picnickers who take advantage of the views afforded whilst enjoying a bite to eat.

Marlborough Road Tube station in St John's Wood, London, was featured in a 1973 BBC television documentary presented by Sir John Betjeman when the station building can clearly be seen as an Aberdeen Angus Steak House. In the early years of the twenty-first century this was a Chinese restaurant and today is a substation for the Metropolitan Line.

Marshall Road, Banbury.

Maryhill in Glasgow closed in 1964, although little happened here until the buildings were demolished in 1980 and the Maryhill Shopping Centre was built. However, the platform site remained untouched in the basement area in the hope the line would be reopened. When adjacent land was developed in 1999 it seemed the line could never see the light of day again, yet the demolition of the shopping centre in 2010 again brought the faint hope of the service being revived.

Maud Junction in Aberdeenshire closed in 1965, although reminders of the railway are still evident in the form of the Maud Railway Station Museum, with remains of the turntable and cattle loading platforms still clearly evident.

Melcombe Regis station closed in 1959. This Dorset station then saw a provender store for the cross-Channel ferries built on the forecourt. Just two years later a repair shop for goods lorries was added. In 1985 these were demolished and by 1999 everything on the site had been cleared, including the go-kart track which had stood alongside the platform for many years. In 2000 the Swannery Retirement Home complex was constructed here.

Melton Constable in Norfolk was cleared in 1971 and a telephone exchange built in its place. Once the telephone exchange was a landmark building in towns and cities but the digital age has made these redundant. Ornamental spandrels, once holding up the station roof, can still be seen doing a similar job at a bus shelter on Fakenham Road. The stations water tower is the most obvious remnant from the railway works and sidings, the area now an industrial estate. Close inspection will reveal repairs to shrapnel damage from an air raid during the Second World War.

Millers Dale is now on the Monsal Trail in Derbyshire. There are two viaducts here, one still used for the trail, and many of the station buildings are still visible. However, aside from the stationmaster's house, now a private residence, the other buildings are only used as toilets – officially, that is.

Mill Hill station in London closed in 1964. Today the only reminder of the railway is the bridge over the former line. Flats have been built on the site, a site covered by material excavated by those building slip roads giving access to the nearby M1 motorway.

Melton Constable station. (*Courtesy of Dr Ben Brooksbank*)

Midland Road and Sutton Coldfield Town station is now a Post Office sorting depot.

Midland Road and Sutton Coldfield Town station's – one platform is still evident alongside the tracks.

Mitcheldean Road station in Herefordshire is now home to a small housing estate. The only remaining clue as to it ever being associated with the railway is its name. Noden Drive recalls Reginald 'Dick' Noden, who was stationmaster here from the end of the Second World War until closure of the station in 1964.

Molyneux Brow station near Bury, Greater Manchester, closed in June 1931. No remains can be found today as the site has given way to the M60 motorway.

Morecambe Promenade station in Lancashire is now the tourist information office and an entertainment centre known as the Platform. To the rear is a retail estate; a Morrison's car park sits where the former goods yard used to be.

Approaching the southernmost and longest tunnel on the Monsal Trail. The cutting at this end contrasts markedly with the breathtaking views from Headstone Viaduct (below), as the Monsal Trail emerges from the hillside.

Morecambe's former goods yard is now the car park for Morrisons.

Morecambe's station has become the tourist information office and entertainment venue known as the Old Platform.

Mortehoe and Woolacombe station in Devon closed in 1970. After years of neglect the place was transformed into the children's theme park *Once Upon a Time*. Former rolling stock contained a number of animations of children's fairytales and the site boasted a number of rides. The attraction, aimed at small children, was sold off in 2005 and later developed as an affordable housing scheme.

Muthill, Perth and Kinross closed in 1964 and was subsequently cleared. A handful of private residences have been built here alongside the offices of a business growing, and even exporting, potatoes.

Nawton in North Yorkshire is now a private residence. However its interesting history demands inclusion in the book. Many entries were omitted to afford those living there some privacy, but the current owners will already be aware it is on record that this station doubled as the village fish and chip shop, in what had been the office of the weighbridge. Later the village blacksmith took up residence and, following his departure, it took on a fourth very different image when the village post office was set up here. Few stations can have had more varied uses than Nawton.

New Hadley Halt was demolished in 1986, effectively replaced by the opening of Telford Central the day after it closed. Small signs of the station remain, particularly when viewed from the footpath on the Haybridge Road side. However, cross the road and locate the triangle of apparent wasteland between the newly built houses and find an area quite clearly designated as a dog's toilet which, for some unfathomable reason, has a gate which is bolted from the outside.

Newport station on the Isle of Wight was demolished long ago and the site is now home to a funeral parlour.

Station House, Nawton – where the new development is known as The Sidings.

Old site of New Hadley Halt.

Newport Pagnall in Buckinghamshire may have closed in 1967 but the buildings and platform can still be made out, although today the site is home to a number of small offices.

Nine Elms station in London saw just ten years working life, mainly because the service did not serve central London and journeys had to be completed by road; it closed in 1848. The site is easily traced because it is now home to the flower section of New Covent Garden when it opened in 1974.

North Wootton station in Norfolk has seen the station become a private residence with the goods yard now the headquarters of both the scouts and guides of North Wootton.

Norwich City station is slowly being uncovered by a group calling themselves Friends of Norwich City Station. While the traffic island situated where the A147, Barnes Road, and St Crispin's Road converge is the central point, the station covered a significant area. Already the wall of platform one and a loading bay area have been revealed and the volunteers' aim is to produce a memorial garden with suitable signs, old images of the station and benches.

Newport Pagnell where the station building is now utilised as offices.

Nottingham Carrington Street station closed in 1848 and yet the site of the station is clearly marked today by Nottingham Magistrates Court.

Nottingham London Road station closed in 1972 and, despite a damaging fire in 1996, the building still stands and first housed a Holmes Place health and fitness club and latterly a Virgin Active Health Club.

Nottingham Victoria closed in 1967 and is now the site of the Victoria Shopping Centre. However the station's clock tower was incorporated into the new building. It is impossible to miss this feature as it is 256ft high.

Oldbury in the West Midlands saw its station closed in 1915, although the branch line remained open for goods until the late 1960s when construction of the M5 motorway effectively severed Oldbury's link to the rail network.

Old Dalby in Leicestershire closed in 1968 and thereafter the track here was used for testing by British Rail. Both the original version of the Advanced Passenger Train and its successor, the Pendolino, were both developed on this site. In July 1984 this was also the site of a staged accident where a diesel locomotive hauling three coaches was deliberately crashed at 100mph into a Flatrol wagon loaded with 'nuclear waste' and lying on its side across the track. With radioactive waste being transported by rail it was to demonstrate that, even in the event of a crash, the nuclear waste flask would remain intact.

Otterham in Cornwall closed in 1966 and while today a part of the site has been developed for private housing, for much of the interim period it was home to a caravan park.

Ottery St Mary in Devon closed in 1967. Today the station building is used by the local youth club, while to the rear there is a small industrial estate, home

Old Freightliner Terminal at Windsor Street in Birmingham, under the shadow of the gasholder, is still a source of power.

Old Station Nursery at Faringdon.

to a local co-operative called Recycling In Ottery (RIO), which encourages residents not to discard their unwanted items but bring them here in the hope others will find use for them. Proceeds go to useful local causes.

Old Station Road, Eynsham.

Ottery St Mary station, now a youth club and the rear dedicated to RIO 'Recycling In Ottery'.

Oswestry's old station doubles as a heritage railway centre and home to several small business outlets.

Padstow in Cornwall closed in 1967. The station building is still here, and was home to a cycle hire shop for those travelling on the Camel Trail, itself the line's former trackbed. However, today this provides a base of operations for Padstow Town Council.

Peak Forest in Derbyshire closed in 1967 and the station buildings are now utilised as offices.

Penmaenpool in Gwynedd closed in 1965. The line lifted and is now a footpath and cycle path known as the Mawddach Trail. The station buildings

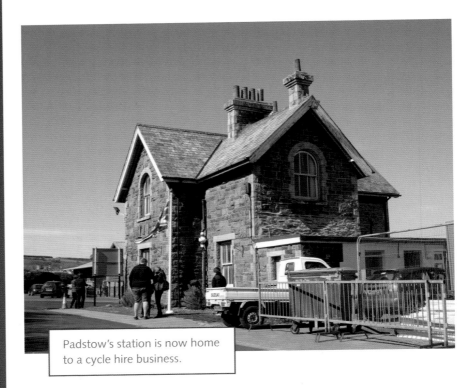

Padstow's station is now home to a cycle hire business.

have been utilised as extensions of the George Hotel, opposite which the local signal still stands. This would have been controlled by the signal box, itself now used as an observation point and information centre by the Royal Society for the Protection of Birds – it gives wonderful views over the nature reserve of the widening estuary.

Penworth Cop Lane in Lancashire closed in 1964 and the line was lifted, this gave local youths an opportunity to use the cutting as an impromptu site for cycle scrambling – a short-lived but creative idea.

Petworth in West Sussex saw the station building converted for use as a guest house. The former Pulman coaches brought here from Marazion in Cornwall have been adapted to provide further accommodation.

Pill in Somerset closed in the 1960s. However, the goods yard was briefly associated with trains once more when in 1984, the BBC comedy series *The Young Ones* filmed the episode entitled *Bambi* which featured Vyvyan being decapitated when leaning out of the carriage window.

Plashetts station in Northumberland is now home to fish. Not a large aquarium, but a site now wholly submerged by Kielder Water.

Plumtree station in Nottinghamshire has survived and is now home to Perkins Restaurant.

Pocklington in Yorkshire closed in 1965 but the station building, now given Grade II listing, is used as a the sports hall by neighbouring Pocklington School.

Pontrilas in Herefordshire has a small business unit operating near the signalbox, still in use for the line here. One small company operates largely on-line (OnTracks.co.uk), supplying parts and equipment for model railways, both nationally and internationally.

Possil in Glasgow closed in 1964 and the yard has long been used as a scrapyard. The station is a Grade C listed building and, while empty and derelict for the last decade, once housed a bookmaker's premises from the 1980s.

The old station site at Pill, the goods yard would have stood opposite the point where the present line turns off to the left.

Potton in Bedfordshire saw its station purchased and refurbished by a former railway man. However, here it is the goods shed which has been converted into a vegetable store.

Primrose Hill station in London has just two reminders of the former railway. The station building is today a local shop, while the former turntable shed is now an entertainment venue appropriately known as the Roundhouse.

Ramsey North in Cambridgeshire is now occupied by Ramsey Auction Rooms.

Ravenscar is best known for what was never here. The train service brought visitors to a coastline that had previously only been seen by fishermen, and tourists were restricted to either Scarborough or Whitby. The railway was seen as the catalyst for expansion at Ravenscar and plans were laid out to develop a brand new resort here. Roads were cut, sewers installed, and homes were built. But the distance from here to the beach deterred visitors and the venture failed. The houses and the streets, although somewhat overgrown, are still visible. The station still exists, alongside the cycle and walking path known as the Cinder Trail. The railway has also left its mark on the map in the form of the only surviving street name in Ravenscar, that of Station Square.

Raydon Wood in Suffolk closed to passengers in 1932, although goods continued until 1965. The station building is now home to a coal merchant's depot.

Rayne station in Essex has changed little since it was built in the 1860s. Freight, in the form of wheat, hay, straw, milk, coal and livestock, and passengers passed through here until the station closed in 1971. In 2004 an

Ravenscar and the remains of former station overlook Station Square.

This advertisement for Ravenscar failed to bring in the crowds.

enterprising group of volunteers began to turn the then derelict buildings and surrounding woodland into something which can be enjoyed by everyone. With guidance from Country Park Rangers the area alongside the former trackbed, now a footpath and cycle path, has been managed to bring back many endangered wildlife species to the area. Today bats, butterflies, great crested newts and dormice can find a safe habitat also enjoyed by nature lovers.

Rayne where the station building would still be easily recognised 150 years after it was built.

Rayne again and aside from the coloured sign, nothing has changed on the platform side.

Redbrook-on-Wye station in the Forest of Dean, Gloucestershire, closed and all traces were removed apart from the viaduct which took the line across the Wye and into Wales. It was probably because this marked the border that the crossing remained intact, serving walkers and cyclists, while the views afforded across the valley encouraged the building of a restaurant on the former station site. The Penallt Viaduct was named for the village on the Welsh side of the Wye.

Riccall in North Yorkshire has no obvious signs of ever having had a railway, although the trackbed is still in daily use as it lies beneath the tarmac of what is now the A19, bypassing the village.

Richmond in North Yorkshire closed but retained most of the buildings. In November 2007, they were reopened as The Station, a complex offering two cinema screens, a restaurant, café, art gallery, heritage centre, several rooms for public hire, and a number of speciality organic food producers.

Richmond's old station.

Rifle Range Platform in Cornwall has one of the strangest histories. Originally it was opened to serve, as the name suggests, a target range for the army – indeed the stop was known colloquially simply as The Target. With the railway the only means of access, troops arrived to hone the skills required when seeing action in both the Boer War and the First World.

While the troops continued to use the cinder platform until 1947, not a shot was fired on the range shortly after the Armistice was signed in 1918. Even more bizarrely the site still exists today and has the railway signs we would expect to find – yet these are a quite modern addition for no signs were ever erected to mark the stop while the track to here was in use.

Ringley Road station near Bury, Greater Manchester, closed in 1953. The station is still here as part of the Irwell Sculpture Trail, a 30-mile trail and the largest public art scheme in England.

Rocester in Staffordshire is today dominated by the factory of J.C. Bamford, better known as the initials JCB, now used to refer to the versatile excavator.

Ringstead and Addington in Northamptonshire found a use for the old sleepers – as stepping stones on a muddy lane.

Such may well have been used to clear the station site, yard and turntable now occupied by the social club and its car park. The line of the railway can still be made out, to the south leading to the home of the angling club, to the north the massive building which houses J. C. Bamford Excavators Ltd.

They are also used by the swans to construct a nest at the appropriately named Swanley Lakes.

Rocester's goods yard and former turntable are now home to the J.C. Bamford social club.

Romsey in Hampshire is now home to a Waitrose supermarket and, in the car park outside, home to a monthly farmers' market where burgers made from the meat of local water buffalo are cooked and savoured.

Ross-on-Wye in Herefordshire was redeveloped as an industrial estate. It is quite easy to make out the goods shed and particularly the engine shed which now houses the indoor part of a garden centre.

Rotherham Masborough in South Yorkshire saw most of the buildings demolished in the 1990s. However, the track is still in use, as are the platforms, although no passenger or freight trains stop here. If they did travellers would be able to visit the main station building where they could enjoy a curry as it is now an Indian restaurant.

Rotherham Westgate in South Yorkshire closed but remained untouched for some twenty years. The local market, which set up each week opposite the station, used the wooden station buildings to house the market stalls after dismantling. Later a Post Office sorting office was built here, the remainder utilised by a scrap metal dealer.

Rothienorman in Aberdeenshire has seen the site cleared and a primary school now stands in its place.

Ross-on-Wye's garden centre is easily recognised as a former engine shed.

Rowfant in West Sussex may have closed in 1967, but both the site and its buildings are not only intact but in constant use by a company who specialise in building roads.

Rowthorn Tunnel at Glapwell in Derbyshire closed many years ago and is now filled in. However, during the Second World War this was used as a storage facility for munitions and had previously found new life as a mushroom farm.

Rudgwick in West Sussex has seen the trackbed become the footpath known as the Downs Link. The unusual sight of a 'bridge over a bridge' has led to the local council installing a viewing platform to allow the public a good view.

Rudgwick Medical Centre, the site of the station and still alongside the former trackbed.

Rudyard station has been recycled as a narrow gauge line.

The old Rugby Central station is now officially a nature reserve, although the trackbed on the left has simply flooded and, at the time of the photograph, absolutely brimful of frogspawn.

Rugby Central station has none of its buildings remaining. The yard, too, has now given way to a modern housing development. However, both trackbed and platforms remain, the former as part of a nature walk and reserve owned by the local council and named the Great Central Way, the latter today serves as an impromptu dam to prevent water from draining, which allows a multitude of frogs to find the perfect place to spawn.

Ruthin in Denbighshire saw its station replaced by Ruthin Craft Centre. A goods crane near the entrance is a reminder of the long-gone railway.

St Ann's in London closed in 1942 as part of war-time cuts and never reopened. Until 2012 the ticket office was used by a newsagent, but has now been demolished.

St German's in Cornwall is still open to trains and passengers, but the siding is no longer accessible from the mainline, despite the rails still holding rolling stock. On the rails stands a travelling post office, no longer where postal workers sort mail on the move but a stationary vehicle which has changed little on the exterior, but inside is very different as it now houses self-catering accommodation of excellent standard.

Yet this is no ordinary piece of rolling stock, this travelling post office is a piece of world railway history. Built in the late nineteenth century, it was rennovated in 1896 when three passenger compartments were removed. Our interest comes from eight years later when, in 1904, it was a part of the train hauled by the *City of Truro* when it made its record-breaking 100mph run, the first time any man had achieved this landmark. Whilst it has a wondrous early history and an exquisite present, the interim period was equally unusual as it became a part of a house in Wales.

Salcey Forest in Northamptonshire is, compared to other former sites, a somewhat ordinary location. Today the single platform is largely intact, albeit hidden from view by the vegetation. The buildings survived until the 1950s, while the trackbed is now a muddy trail running along what is marked as the Midshires Way long-distance trail.

Yet it is not the present-day remains which have resulted in Salcey Forest's inclusion but its history. This was not one of the stations to suffer at the hands of Dr Beeching. Indeed, as we have already noted the buildings were here until the 1950s, however this was sixty years after the station saw its last passenger and more than four decades after the line officially ceased to carry freight.

In truth the opening of this station in December 1892, along with its neighbour Stoke Bruerne, was probably a mistake. Records show the initial service saw just one individual alighting here, with another at Stoke Bruern, although seven did join the service. With four trains each day and a maximum of twenty passengers per week incurring weekly losses of £40 it could not have come as a surprise when the line soon closed. However there is no known shorter service in British railway history, this station having a passenger service for exactly 120 days.

Not that this was the end of Salcey Forest, through traffic continued to travel through here between Avonmouth Docks and Somerstown Goods in the form of banana trains until May 1958. Planned as a temporary closure to allow the construction of a bridge taking the M1 overhead, the line never reopened. Even this did not make the track redundant, for while through trains were no more, the track did provide storage space for condemned coaches waiting to be cut up for scrap.

Sandwell and Banford in Somerset is now the site of a sheltered housing complex, the former station preserved as the offices.

Sandford in Somerset has been developed as a retirement village. The station is quite evident at the centre of the site, while the former engine shed has a modern equivalent alongside, a mirror image of the original which now houses the dining room for the complex. All the roads here take the name of apples, the obvious choice as directly opposite here are the orchards where the Thatchers company grow the apples used in producing their famous cider.

Sawdon in North Yorkshire closed in the 1950s. In recent years it has been refurbished and offers holiday accommodation in a setting where just about everything of the working station still exists, bar the track and the trains.

What will be the New Railway Inn at Sandford, Somerset.

Sandford station retirement village, the dining room designed to appear as the old engine shed.

Schoolhill railway station in Aberdeen has a few tell-tale remnants which can now be seen in the car park adjacent to Her Majesty's Theatre.

Scotsgap in Northumberland has seen the station building and the yard occupied by an agricultural merchant.

Seaton in Rutland, closed in 1966, was cleared and is now home to the local scrapyard.

Semley in Wiltshire closed in 1966 and has been developed as both an industrial estate and a commercial centre.

Sheepbridge in Derbyshire may be closed but it is quite clear a station once existed here. Among the remains are the former booking office, now a television repair shop, and a storage facility for a selection of antiques.

Sheffield Wicker in South Yorkshire is now home to a branch of Tesco Extra. Previously it had been used by a car dealership and, before road changes for the northern relief road, had been where Amanda King's sculpture *Made in Sheffield* stood.

Sheepbridge's former booking office.

Shepton Mallett in Somerset's High Street station has now been relocated by the East Somerset Railway. Prior to this the station building was put to good use as a depot for a cleaning company.

Shipston-on-Stour's railway site is remembered in the road names of the new housing development. Whilst Signal Road, Railway Crescent and The Sidings are clear, perhaps the man deemed responsible should have been Dr Richard Beeching and not Thomas Beecham, the chemist whose name is synonymous with a powder designed to ease colds and flu symptoms.

Shrewsbury Abbey station has seen some changes since it closed in the 1960s. While the station itself was comparatively small, the adjacent yard included a goods and wagon building works. First an oil depot occupied the old works site, until that closed in 1988. It is now a sizable car park. Look to the east of the car park and the old platform is very easy to see, with the station building also visible. At the time of writing there are plans to reopen the station as a tourist information centre and a small café.

Sidmouth in Devon has used the old station as offices, while the station yard has seen every square inch utilised to bring businesses and jobs to the area.

Sidmouth's old station.

The extensive yard at Sidmouth is now home to a large industrial estate.

Silloth in Cumbria closed in 1964, but it was more than forty years before the site was cleared and developed to provide housing for single-parent families.

Singleton in West Sussex has not seen a train stop here for decades, although the buildings remain and are put to good use by the owner of the local vineyard.

Skipworth near York has three railway carriages, all having been refurbished to provide excellent self-catering accommodation.

Slinfold in West Sussex still has a couple of the original railway cottages, while the rest of the station site is now home to a caravan park.

Snettisham in Norfolk has seen the station building become a home, while the engine shed and granary are now utilised by a furniture dealer.

Southampton Terminus station still stands but today houses a casino, while the station's associated hotel has been converted into luxury apartments. Lines can still be seen leading to the glass canopy, the major remnant of the old station.

Soho Benson Road tram stop was once Soho and Winson Green station, Birmingham. Note the main line still runs alongside.

Terminus station in Southampton, now a casino.

The glass canopy for platform one of Southampton Terminus station is still intact, while beneath it rails are still visible among the cobbles.

Southfleet near Dartford in Kent has seen the stationmaster's house become a private residence, with the site of the station building now occupied by a private tennis court. The trackbed was relaid in 1998 and now sees more passengers and realises more revenue than it ever could hope to as part of the Gravesend branch line as it carries traffic on the Channel Tunnel Rail Link.

South Kentish Town tube station in London has seen the station building taken as a branch of the *Cash Converters* chain.

Southport Eastgate Street station closed in 1851, although the trains continued to run past, as indeed they do to this day. The ticket office and the stationmaster's house survive, the latter now let to the Southport Model Railway Society.

Southport Lord Street station closed in the 1950s and soon afterwards the station site became home to Ribble Buses. The station building, with its impressive clock tower, remained unchanged. While the buses departed twenty years ago, the front of the building is still unchanged, and inside a Morrison's supermarket is trading.

South Shields station in Tyneside is now the site of a Shopmobility centre, the new building designed in a similar style to the station. Some of the site is still used by the Newcastle Metro system.

Southwater in West Sussex closed in 1966. While the track is now a part of the Downs Way footpath, the station site is home to Horsham District Council's offices.

Speech House Road in the Forest of Dean, Gloucestershire, has been a footpath and cycle way for some years. A station sign still exists marking the approximate location, while plans by the Dean Forest Heritage Railway could eventually see trains travel the 2 miles to Speech House Road once more.

Staines High Street station is no more. The whole site is buried beneath a sprawling multi-storey car park. Yet the trains still run past the site along the same line.

Staines West in Moor Lane can still be recognised as the main station building, now occupied by the offices of more than one company. However,

Speech House Road station site, the trackbed is now a footpath and cycle path.

Staines from the multi-storey with the tracks still visible in the distance.

The old Staines West station building.

it is behind the building where we focus, for the current car park includes rails still visible flush with the surface, while outside the entrance is a few feet of rail and sleepers in front of buffers rescued from the site.

Stamford Bridge in Yorkshire closed in 1965. The station is still here and houses a private members club serving this village.

Stanhoe in Norfolk closed in 1959 and many of the buildings remain in good condition. The area has been known as Station Farm since closure.

Staveley in Derbyshire has seen its station replaced by Erin Road (A9192). Following this south-east will bring road users to junction 29A of the M1.

Steyning in West Sussex stands on the Downs Link footpath, but it is the old warehousing here that interests us having been converted into living accommodation.

Stixwould in Lincolnshire has changed little. Aside from the removal of the rails and ballast, the platforms, station sign, trackbed and station building remain. Today the line is Water Rail Way cycle and footpath, while the station has been converted into the guest house called Time Away.

Stockport Tiviot in Lancashire closed in 1967 and the site was developed as offices and a supermarket.

Stoke St Gregory never had a railway station in its entire history until the line closed. It was then the station at nearby Athelney was moved in its entirety to the playing fields at Stoke St Gregory where it now acts as the pavilion for the village cricket team and local tennis enthusiasts.

Sturminster Newton in Dorset closed in 1966. While a trading estate now occupies the site, its history is marked by commemorative gates proudly proclaiming this had been a part of the Somerset and Dorset Joint Railway.

Swansea and the name of the Mount railway station may not be instantly recognised by railway enthusiasts. Its location is easy to find, simply standing outside the entrance to Swansea Museum and one is standing on the line itself. This route was opened in 1807, not a misprint but the first recorded passenger railway service and station anywhere in the world – horse-drawn, of course. The Oystermouth Railway was originally to bring coal and iron ore to Swansea.

Stoke St Gregory's cricket and tennis pavilion.

Symonds Yat station has its tea rooms and pub using the old platform as foundations.

Swansea Victoria has been cleared and is now where the Swansea Leisure Centre stands.

Symonds Yat in Herefordshire stands on the banks of the Wye. Here the idyllic surroundings attract numerous visitors each year, some coming by road, others on foot or bicycle, while there are always those who arrive by boat, be it their own or by virtue of the ferry, not rowed but tethered to a rope spanning the river and hauled across by the ferryman.

Once the railway brought visitors here and some may not realise the buildings on the right bank stand on the former platform. Here inside you'll find a public house and neighbouring tea rooms that display images of the line and the station before its closure in January 1959.

Tattershall station in Lincolnshire has been home to a gallery for some years. Here a talented individual produces a range of hand-thrown pottery and paintings, the latter do feature the odd railway theme.

Tavistock North in Devon closed in 1968 and remains an impressive sight. The viaduct at Tavistock alone covered five spans of 50ft each and three more of 32ft, crossing several streets. The station covered around 5 acres and is the second largest on the former line. The station buildings noticeably differed, with walls of granite from Dartmoor and roofs of slate from Mill Hill Quarry.

In 1968, five years after Dr Beeching's report, the station may have closed to railway business, but the stationmaster and his wife continued to live here, even renaming their home – remembering it was still railway property – Beeching's Folly! 'Snowy' Hooper, so called because of his shock of white hair, refused to believe the railway would never return, continuing to maintain the buildings and ensure when the next train stopped here, the disembarking passengers would find a station with clean paint, sparkling windows, and a show of flowers when the season demanded. For three years Mr Hooper steadfastly refused to believe his beloved station had closed, but the sad truth finally dawned when, in 1971, the lines were finally lifted and no trains could come here.

Sometime afterwards the Hoopers were offered the chance to purchase their home from British Rail. Delighted by the proposal, they quickly accepted. Later came the opportunity to buy the 5 acres of the goods yard, now home to the local council, which included the magnificent viaduct. Hooper declined, despite the price of just £1. Not a businessman, he failed to see the enormous profit which could have been his from the goods yard to the east, however he did understand that it would be his responsibility to pay for the repair and upkeep of the viaduct should he take up the offer.

The station is now privately owned but the rest of the property has been sold off for development, and English Heritage and the Sustrans project have taken care to ensure this colossus still dominates the skyline above the north of the town. After the track was lifted, the former trackbed became a route for walkers and cyclists, and in 1999 a private sale of the station buildings resulted in them receiving a Grade II listing.

In 2007 the buildings were purchased by the current owners, Jenny and Colin Rogers, who turned the property into three exquisite holiday cottages. It is not hard to see that the buildings were once old railway properties as they have been faithfully maintained. However, inside you will find five-star luxury accommodation fit for families of four or more.

Tettenhall in the West Midlands closed in 1932 and the line was eventually lifted thirty-three years later. Unusually the station is still here and hardly changed since it was a working station. Today the waiting room is used as a Park Ranger station.

Thorntone Dale in North Yorkshire became the site of offices used by a firm laying a gas pipeline to Pickering. When this was completed the now empty station was refurbished as three holiday cottages at the centre of a caravan centre.

Tilbury Riverside station in Essex is now used as a covered car park for Tilbury Passenger Terminal.

Tiffield Pocket Park wildlife reserve and walk.

Tinsley station near Sheffield, South Yorkshire, saw part of the trackbed used for the Sheffield Supertram transport service.

Tintern in Monmouthshire closed in 1964 and was subsequently purchased by the local council for the princely sum of £1,500. More money was spent in refurbishment to open the site as a visitor attraction, with a café and an exhibition centre. Old carriages were adapted to show a film about the life of the station. Later the carriages were replaced by others housing a shop and a tourist information office.

Tintern Old Station. (*Courtesy of Amy Rigg*)

Tintern Old Station.
(*Courtesy of Amy Rigg*)

Tipton Five Ways station in the West Midlands closed in 1962. The site was eventually taken over by the car park of Bean Industries and the adjacent factory, although this closed early in the twenty-first century.

Tongham at Guildford in Surrey is long gone and the site is now occupied by the Blackwater Valley Relief Road. Officially designated the A331, it links the A31 to the M3.

Torrington in Devon closed in 1965, although it continued to run for another seventeen years. All the station buildings survive, note in particular those on the Up platform which became the Puffing Billy public house and restaurant. Tracks remain, where a coach, brake van and wagon stand, separated from the Tarka Trail, itself running along the old trackbed, by a fence. Plans to

The Tissington Trail follows the old track, although the obvious dip here indicates where a bridge has been removed.

Access to Ashbourne along the form tunnel from the Tissington Trail, complete with lighting and sounds of an approaching steam train!

relay the track to Bideford have been approved and continue to advance to the stage where short journeys behind a diesel locomotive are possible.

Whilst the property is listed as a public house, it should probably be seen as a licensed restaurant. Inside the walls are festooned with memorabilia examining the station in its heyday, and around its closure. Just how the 'pub' came to be known as the Puffing Billy is unclear. One story speaks of

The Puffing Billy at Torrington.

the original licensee being a heavy smoker named William, although this is unconfirmed.

Trawscoed in Dyfed became the new home of a local coal merchant when the line closed.

Treforest High Level station was on the Barry line, but closure saw the site cleared and it is now home to maintenance centre for police vehicles.

Tunbridge Wells West in Kent is a splendid architectural construction, justifiably afforded Grade II listing in 1986. Initially this became a restaurant in the Beefeater chain known as The Old West Station, later sold to Herald Inns and Bars who continue to offer refreshment as both a pub and a restaurant. What was the goods yard and stabling sidings is now covered in tarmac, serving as a car park and home to a large Sainsbury's supermarket.

Turvey in Bedfordshire has some reminders of the railway, including the station building, which now doubles as the offices of Cargill plc. The rest of the site is used by a multi-national company which trades in energies, agriculture and livestock, food and pharmaceuticals, risk management and raw materials worldwide. With their headquarters in Minnesota the turnover

Thankfully Tunbridge Wells West station has been saved as a restaurant aptly named the Old West station.

of in excess of $130 billion dwarfs the takings of Turvey station, which opened in 1901 to serve a residential district of just 782 individuals. The annual total journeys peaked in 1913 at 13,207.

Twenty station in Lincolnshire closed to passengers in 1959. For some years the station building has been home to a double-glazing workshop.

Verwood in Dorset has seen its former station site put to a number of varied uses. The goods yard is now a residential estate. What had been the booking office, platforms and trackbed is now the B3081, also known as Station Road, while the station building itself stood on land now given over to the beer garden of the Albion Inn.

Wadebridge in Cornwall closed in 1965. The goods shed is now a youth club, while the station building is now identified as the Betjeman Centre. Within there is a large room where many groups meet, a sun lounge, a coffee lounge, a centre for Thai chi, and a hairdressers.

There are many reminders of the former poet inside. His name was given to the centre after he mentioned Wadebridge in his autobiography saying, 'On Wadebridge Station what a breath of sea scented by the Camel Valley! Cornish air, soft Cornish rains, and silence after steam.'

Wadsley Bridge in Sheffield, South Yorkshire, has but one reminder that this was once a railway station. The station name still adorns this site in the shape of the sign that once adorned the signal box, and stands out in what is now the John Fairest Funeral Home.

Wadebridge station.

The John Fairest Funeral Home at Wadsley Bridge.

Walsingham in Norfolk closed in 1964, but before the end of the decade the station buildings were used as a small monastic community for a branch of the Russian Orthodox Church.

Waterhouses in County Durham closed in 1968, and the station site has since been cleared and landscaped as a local park.

Watford Central underground station is now occupied by the Moon Under Water public house, one of the Wetherspoons chain.

Wednesfield station in the West Midlands was cleared after closure and following the lifting of the trackbed has been covered by the A4124 Wednesfield Way.

Wednesfield Heath station in the West Midlands closed in 1965 and demolished within weeks. While the station area has become the nature reserve known as Station Fields, the trackbed has become part of the bypass road.

Wells-next-the-Sea in Norfolk closed in 1964. Shortly afterwards the station building was home to a second-hand bookshop, and the on-site corn mill converted into flats. Today the whole area is an industrial estate.

Wellow in Somerset closed to trains in 1966. Ten years later it was purchased by Peter Blake and his wife, Jann Haworth, who converted it into their home and workplace. They used it as an artist studio and it became known as their Brotherhood of Ruralists period.

Wednesbury Town station in the West Midlands closed in 1964, at the time Wednesbury was still officially a part of Staffordshire. Today the site of the station has been acquired by a waste disposal plant, a concern which had moved on to the station car parks around the turn of the millennium and is steadily growing to take in the whole site.

West Bromwich station in the West Midlands closed in 1972, the site remaining deserted and overgrown. In 1999 the new tram line, known as Midland Metro, was built and the station site was utilised for the new tram station named West Bromwich Central.

Westerham in Kent is now home to an industrial estate, and while the track line is hidden the railway cottages are comfortable homes. At the entrance to the estate can be seen the base of the crane which was operated in the goods yard. This is the Flyers Way Industrial Estate, named after Class H 0-4-4T No. 31518 locomotive *Westerham Flyer*, which pulled the trains on the last day of service, Saturday 26 October 1961.

West Hallam in Derbyshire closed in 1964 and the site is now home to a garden centre.

West St Leonards in East Sussex still has a railway running past the former station. Indeed where the engine sheds once stood is now a facility for washing trains. The rest of the station buildings are long gone and are now occupied by the warehouse and car park for TK Maxx.

Westward Ho! in North Devon has been recycled in many ways since it closed in 1917 – after just sixteen years' operation. The station site itself became a bus station in the 1960s, the signal box doubling as the bus station's snack bar.

Wetherby York Road station in West Yorkshire has been largely demolished and utilised as a commercial estate. However, the engine shed survives, and is easily recognised from outside. Yet, the interior has been greatly refurbished and is now home to a dancing club, with live and recorded music for clients to dance to. Perhaps they will have learned some of their moves

The site of West St Leonards station.

York Road, Wetherby, was an engine shed, but now it houses a dance club.

upstairs where a studio has been created under the eaves to teach those of all ages and abilities.

Wheelock and Sandbach station in Cheshire has had the track removed and now forms part of the National Cycle Nework Route 5, riders passing the station building will notice it is in use by a tyre-fitting company.

Station Stores at Whitmore.

The Health Centre in Whitstable.

Whitstable Harbour site has some remnants which are visible, such as the stables used to house the horses that used shunt the wagons around the harbour. Today those stables house a car showroom. The site of the southern station is now occupied by the local health centre.

Whitwick station.

Whitwick Station first saw life in 1883, although by 1931 regular passenger traffic had ceased. While freight continued to use the line until 1963, it passed a building used as a blacksmith's workshop. Whilst other station buildings were demolished around 1975, the station building itself became home to the newly created Whitwick Historical Group, who refurbished and reopened the site.

Wigan in Lancashire closed in 1964 and it was not until the twenty-first century the site was developed as the Grand Arcade Shopping Centre.

Willington in Bedfordshire may have closed in 1968 but the trackbed later surfaced to become National Cycle Route 51, however hopes for a reinstated railway service remained until quite recently. In 2006 the county council approved plans to bring this part of the Bedfordshire into the world of the Olympic Games with construction of the Bedford Rowing Lake. The lake straddles the trackbed and covers an area of 84 acres and was built at a reputed cost of £40 million. Any decision to reopen the line would now require a bridge to cross the lake and increase the cost significantly, as this would be the second longest railway bridge in Britain, second only to the famous Forth Railway Bridge.

Willoughby in Lincolnshire closed to passengers in 1970. A 1-mile stretch of the former trackbed is now a footpath, one passing through an area designated as a nature reserve. However it is the station's former footbridge which is of particular interest, not that it can be seen here. It was removed and erected at nearby Burgh le Marsh where it allows pedestrians to cross a narrow stretch of a fishing pond.

Wimbourne in Dorset closed in 1964 and demolition followed soon after. It is now home to Wimbourne's weekly market.

Wingham in Kent is where the former sidings were located, as evidenced by the name of the Old Station Farm Shop.

Winscombe station in Somerset was cleared years ago, the site is now a part of the Cheddar Valley Walk known as Millennium Green.

Winslow in Buckinghamshire closed to passengers in 1968, although the line remained open until 1993. Shortly after closure a pigsty was erected across the trackbed, this was later to become part of the kennels currently occupying the site. Just how long the dogs will be in residence is unclear as there are plans to reopen the line in 2019.

The Old Station Farm Shop at Wingham, Kent.

Woodstock station and yard has been redeveloped.

Wisbech East in Cambridgeshire is today covered by a housing development. However, shortly after the closure of the railway, the station was cleared, and it became home to the Octavia Hill Centre for the disabled. Meanwhile the goods yard was purchased by Purina, who built a factory here.

Wolferton in Norfolk would probably have been either a halt or request stop were it not for the regular traffic of royal trains. As the nearest station to Sandringham it opened in 1862, the same year that the Prince of Wales bought the Sandringham estate, and closed in 1969. During its operational years innumerable trains arrived here – between 1884 and 1911 alone some 645 trains brought royal passengers to Norfolk.

Following closure, railwayman Eric Walker bought the sight, reopening it the following year as a museum displaying more than 6,000 items of royal and railway memorabilia. It was later inherited by Eric's son and sold on in 2001. Both the station building and the signal box have been given Grade II listings.

Wolverhampton Low Level station in the West Midlands closed to passenger traffic in the 1970s and freight the following decade. Whilst the site was levelled in 2006 the station building, having Grade II listing, still stands.

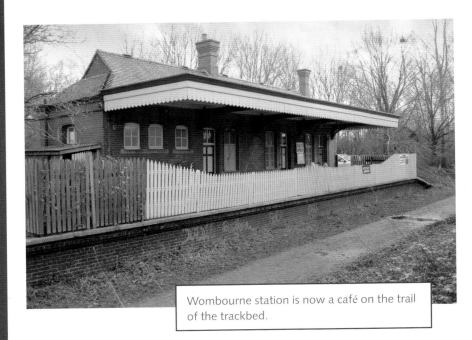

Wombourne station is now a café on the trail of the trackbed.

Initially there were plans to turn this into a casino, but this failed to come to fruition. Until the summer of 2010 it housed an art gallery, and since has been refurbished as a banqueting hall.

Woodford Halse in Northamptonshire closed in 1966 and was later home to a sales centre for touring caravans.

Woodford Halse has seen the buildings put to good use.

The station site is now occupied by a timber yard.

The trackbed offers space for a local funfair to over-winter!

Wyvale garden centre looking along the line of the track.

Wootton Bassett in Wiltshire has seen the southern approach adapted to lead to the stone distribution depot of Foster Yeoman. The limestone, from the Mendip Hills in Somerset, still arrives by train to a remaining siding. While the siding runs alongside, the access to it means running past and coming off at Chippenham before returning.

Yarmouth South Town station in Norfolk eventually closed in 1970. Whilst it has been cleared and redeveloped (it is covered by the A12 link road), initially the station and its buildings were used as the headquarters of an oil company.

Yeovil's station and yard has become the cinema and retail park.

Yeovil closed in 1967 and the site was cleared. For many years this was a car and a coach park, while recent development has seen a cinema and leisure centre being constructed here.

York Old Station in North Yorkshire has recently seen a complete reconstruction job and the site is now home to the headquarters of the City of York Council.

Tintern station sign in the correct Great Western Railway colours. (*Courtesy of Amy Rigg*)

If you enjoyed this book, you may also be interested in …

ANTHONY POULTON-SMITH

BEECHING
50 Years On

978 0 7524 8092 3

Visit our website and discover thousands of other History Press books.

www.thehistorypress.co.uk

The History Press